"*Lighten Your Heart: Healing Psalms of Bugs and Beasts* is a refreshing book. It is a flight of fancy, an adult's negotiation with his childhood and contemplative spirit. I find the book peaceful, a perfect solace at the end of a turbulent day. William Cleary's heart sings and rejoices, a heart pure enough for the beatitudes and big enough to take in all creation. It is not a long distance from poems to psalms to parables to God. William Cleary closes the gap with a leap of grace and a creative dance."

Dr. Anthony T. Padovano
Theologian, Author, Playwright

"Cleary's *Healing Psalms* are wonderful entry points into prayer and meditation. Delightful and insightful, these 'psalms of bugs and beasts' find us where we live and express what is deepest in our hearts. Every parish should have a hundred copies of this playful, prayerful little book."

Thomas Hart, Author
Hidden Spring: The Spiritual Dimension of Therapy

"*Lighten Your Heart: Healing Psalms of Bugs and Beasts* is a great gift. This lyrical chorus of creation reminds us that every creature is indeed a voice of the Divine. This book is imaginative, entertaining, and profound. I recommend it."

Jim Conlon
Author, *Earth Story, Sacred Story*

"St. Thomas Aquinas said that the two main sources of divine revelation are the Bible and nature. Bill Cleary is a genius at illuminating the way each animal, from the inchworm to the kangaroo, yearns to help us on our journey as it shares its special and delightful voice of divine revelation with us."

Dennis, Sheila and Matthew Linn
Re-Member Ministries

"William Cleary swings open the door of the Ark and parades a delightful group of creatures before us in these fresh, witty, and wise prayer-poems. Celebrate, he tells us, the dance of creation and it will reveal the surprising rhythms of your own heart. I found myself thoroughly entranced by the music and became an eager stowaway, smiling and singing along."

Wayne Simsic
Author, *Songs of Sunrise, Seeds of Prayer*

"This book is written in the profound tradition of Francis of Assisi. It teases out of us an attention to ourselves unavailable in more serious theological or spiritual works. Cleary's images and playful 'critter meditations' will bring personal insights to light long after reading. This is a great prayer book to have with your morning coffee!"

Bill Huebsch
Author, *A Spirituality of Wholeness:*
The New Look at Grace

"*Lighten Your Heart* takes us all back to an earlier time when our ancestors recognized the animals and birds as intimate friends, partners in the community of sun and moon, earth and sky. In Cleary's psalms and vivid poetry, bugs and beasts speak of our very human foibles and hidden talents. Any reader will be transformed by the power of Cleary's words and his wisdom of the heart."

Dr. Ed Sellner
Author, *Soul-Making* and *Wisdom of the Celtic Saints*

Lighten Your Heart

William Cleary

TWENTY-THIRD PUBLICATIONS
Mystic, CT 06355

Twenty-Third Publications
185 Willow Street
P.O. Box 180
Mystic, CT 06355
(203) 536-2611
800-321-0411

ISBN 0-89622-650-6
Library of Congress Catalog Card Number 95-60090
Printed in the U.S.A.

Dedication

To a lifelong friend,
a buddy,
whose awesome talent
and sweet wit
have often
lightened my heart.

Contents

Introduction   1

Armadillo
   A prayer of assurance that God loves and cares for us   4

Butterfly   6
   A joyous psalm of lighthearted hope

Chicken   8
   A prayerful invitation to lay our fears on God

Dragonfly   10
   A cry for help in our moments of depression

Elephant   12
   A prayer for those who feel awkward and ugly

Firefly   14
   A song of delight for the darkness of night

Goat   16
   A joyous salute to risk and adventure

Hummingbird   18
   A hymn of praise from one of God's tiniest creatures

Inchworm   20
   A psalm of hope for the future

Junebug   22
   A jubilant song in praise of resurrection

Kangaroo   24
   A prayer of thanksgiving and trust

Ladybug   26
   A humorous lament of indignation

Meadowlark 28
A big prayer of praise from a small voice

Nuthatch 30
A plea from a searcher of the truth

Octopus 32
A song of happy self-acceptance

Parrot 34
A psalm of sorrow for "human" failings

Quail 36
A querulous request for more time, more life

Raccoon 38
A joyous hymn of thanks and self-acceptance

Snail 40
A gentle reminder to pray before sleep

Turkey 42
A psalm of distress for those who feel down

Unicorn 44
A prayerful celebration of existence

Vulture 46
A prayerful promise to change and grow

Worm 48
A conversion prayer for workaholics

Xema 50
A joyous ode to life and love

Yak 52
A prayerful reminder not to "name-call"

Zebra 54
A lighthearted invitation to laugh at life

Author's Notes 56

Afterword by Noah 63

Introduction

Animals are quite helpful to me. Fish, birds, worms—
they move through water, air, and earth with the greatest of
ease. It's inspiring. My own life gets hectic, absurd, painful,
embarrassing at times. Meanwhile non-human creatures
great and small carry on as if everything's okay.

Should I be a clown? Okay, says the stinkbug, the cen-
tipede, the parrot. Should I be content with living in the
dark? I submit, says the noble bat and the patient firefly. Is
Death knocking on the door? Let it happen, says the Mayfly
who lives less than 24 hours. As I said, it's inspiring.

I have always loved Carmen Bernos De Gasztold's classic
Prayers From the Ark, first published half a century ago. Her
animal prayers are not only inspiring, but are often healing
as well.

Not long ago a painful experience challenged my imagination and made me aware of the value of healing prayers. I

found myself all alone and surrounded by thirty "superior" men and women, every one with a Ph.D. but me. There was no place to hide. I looked around the conference table, hoping I would not be noticed. A Great Debate was going on, and profound insights and impenetrable principles abounded. I had nothing to contribute, and I felt both lost and dimwitted.

Escaping after 36 hours, on my departing plane I tried—in the presence of God—to make sense of what had happened. What had it been like, really? I know! I felt like a turkey. And then I heard the turkey in me praying. (See page 42.) I began to laugh. The stranger in the seat next to me moved nervously. I tried to control my glee. Out the window the Pittsburgh airport slid into view.

I changed planes, heading now for Vermont. I began feeling strong, my truer self again. It was all so foolish, of course. Why had I felt so intimidated, so shamed, so disoriented by that circle of experts?

Was it because childhood wounds had not healed, and were subconsciously being rubbed raw again? Humiliations repressed out of consciousness, pushed down and out of sight—were they still there, to give me discomfort?

Whatever the reason, the turkey medicine had healed me. The laughter in my heart had softened the sorrow and soothed away the hurt with a healing balm of understanding and perspective.

I rejoiced to realize I was not simply a dumpster of those negative feelings. I was all my feelings, including a respectable strain of human determination that was also part of my inner self. Aha! What healing image from the critter world could help me take on my truer, my never-surrendering self? Suddenly an amiable goat took shape in my head and he too began to pray. (See page 16.)

It made me smile. By the time our plane banked down over a darkened Lake Champlain, I was back together. I was healed. I guess there is medicine in animals, as Native Americans have always told us: medicine, revelation, humor, astonishment, even holiness and mystery.

The minute I "hear" one or other of my critter friends at prayer (there are twenty-six who pray in this collection), a sense of the Divine Presence mushrooms up in me, a rainbow streaks across the sky, illusions dim out, and the astonishing technicolor real takes shape.

I begin to see a horizon through the dark scrim of clouds, and I get the feeling (like Noah must have had) that we are going to make it. Together.

I hope these prayers have the same effect on you. See if you recognize yourself anywhere among them. Perhaps they will heal and lighten (and even enlighten) your heart as they always have mine.

William Cleary, Shelburne, Vt.

The Plea of a Devout Armadillo

Look down, dear God, see what I did?
I heard You coming—so I hid!
    Forgive me for my fear of woe,
    But life is full of war, you know.

My friends and I all dress like tanks,
Thick armor plates protect our flanks,
    When fox or badger start a brawl,
    We roll up like an iron ball.

In trying times óur worst nightmare
Would be to give in to despair.
    Your Word, that "purpose" fills the world,
    Avoids the need to live encurled.

The truth is, God, Your care and word
Assure us pain is not absurd,
    And give us hope, when hope seems gone,
    For standing fast and holding on.

But Armadillos often have
No choice, short of being bit in half,
  To hide awhile, till we discern
  That God shares in our worst concern.

So though I wear this coat of steel,
I know, God, that your Care is real,
  Your Love built into all our fates
  Is safer far than armored plates.

A Butterfly's Beatitude

I dive into the sunshine,
   I dance across the air,
I glorify the afternoon
   And ridicule despair.

My wings a sunny yellow
   Or wild design of gold,
I hint of hope for all the things
   That prophets have foretold:

   A better world is coming!
      There's room on earth for all!
   Be fruitful and creative!
      God loves both great and small!

So happiness and promises
   And justice I will sing,
Though I am just a lowly bug,
   I proudly do my thing.

O Wondrous God of color,
   Receive my thanks, I pray,
That I can have so great a role
   Though I live but just this day.

The Chills of
a Chicken Chicken

Should I put all my fears aside?
Am I too quickly terrified?
  When farmer begs,
  I lay my eggs!
(Is he plotting chickencide,
To sell me to Kentucky Fried?)

Oh, dear, what myriad fears are mine!
At every noise I screech and whine
    O God of All,
    Please hear my call!
Don't let me end a trembling mess
Of dread, suspicion, fear and stress.

Yes, cowards die a thousand deaths,
Courageous folks but once! Still, breaths
    Of threatened ills
    Give me the chills,
Of doom and gloom, while dangers loom,
And every step leads to the tomb!

Born a chicken, I can't change,
My chicken heart so shy and strange,
    Easy to scare:
    Look out! Beware!
These warnings spook me through and through!
I'm scared of my own shadow too!

God, can we lay these fears on you?
Ask that you even feel them too?
    Learn how to cope,
    Learn how to hope,
Knowing your love will see us through?
Don't chicken out! We're trusting you.

The Dragonfly's Depression

Ancient Wisdom ever new!
Behold your creature feeling blue,
Depressed, disheartened, cheerless, down,
With somber eyes and joyless frown.

I'm born to fly and levitate
While in my arms I hold my mate,
She loves to soar and dive and race
For miles and miles in my embrace.

Instead, a gloom pervades my heart,
My energies refuse to start,
And why? No reason: just the weight
Of life and death and pain and fate.

Great God of life, your way is best,
I know at heart my life is blessed,
So I'll endure this night of gloom
Till morning flowers start to bloom.

Meantime I'll keep faith undefiled
    And hope—because I'm Wisdom's child—
For all the joy and inner glow
That flying dragons ought to know. 🀄

The Large Sighs of an Elephant

Some people laugh and say I'm oversize,
   O God most high,
Some say weird is my trunk, too bold my eyes.
   I want to cry.

My tusks stick out, my feet bizarre and flat,
   My skin too tough,
My walk too slow, my legs too long and fat.
   I've had enough!

Make me a horse, dear God, make me a deer,
   Some noble thing,
So I can fly and race while people cheer
   And I'm the king.

And while I wait for answers to this prayer,
   I ask again,
Then hear the sweet mysterious silence there—
   And sigh Amen.

A Firefly's Affirmation

Creator of both night and day,
I do not understand your way,
    The other fireflies and I
    See many things that mystify.

Oh, yes, we're glad to be alive,
Of course, and love to glow and thrive,
    It's fun from darkest night till dawn
    To flash and twinkle on the lawn.

But we are horrified of day
When we must put our lamps away
    And close our eyes and cease our fun
    Till nightfall drives away the sun.
What kind of horrid creatures play
In daylight? Can they see their way?

O God of Every Mystery,
Give us clear eyes so we can see
   How any world of wonder must
   Have room for other things than us,
Strange things that love the light of day!
And while we're sleeping, wake and play!

The Heart of a Goat with Gumption

Tie me to a wagon,
    I'll pull it till I'm sore,
But in my heart of hearts I know
    I'm made for something more.

A lowly "Goat" they call me,
    But, God, you know my dreams,
I long to climb the highest peaks
    And leap the wildest streams.

In truth, I am Adventure,
    Ambition, Risk, and Dream,
More bold than ox or sheep or cow
    With richer milk and cream.

There's nothing that can bind me,
    I'll butt until I'm free
Through fence or wall till I become
    Who I was meant to be.

Hymn of a Hummingbird

Small is beautiful, they say,
Creator, do you feel that way?
    You've made hummingbirds so wee!
    Some of us small as a bumble bee,
With eggs the size of navy beans,
And nests too small to fit sardines!

Wing-speed's the boast you'll hear from us
At 70 flaps per second plus,
    So fast most eyes can't even see,
    But not, quick-eyed God, too fast for thee:
(Your Spirit's wings are hardly less:
Seventy times seven at least, I'd guess.)

Rainbows of fiery reds and greens
Yellows and orange in glittering sheens
    Color our coats with a sparkling hue,
    Though we're too fast for a steady view,
Darting the deep-throated flowers among,
Sipping their sweets with our straw-centered tongue.

Your love for us helps build our worth
Since 400 kinds you've created on earth,
   In heaven, we know you will need us perforce
   Since heavenly choirs can use hummers, of course,
So, God, how about a small standing ovation
For the tiniest squirt of a bird in creation?

An Inchworm's
Alleluia

Dear God, is any bug more calculating
    Than are we inchworms, shyly tiptoeing,
Measuring our steps, so we will know the number
    Of thanks we owe for your empowering?

We may not move as fast as others do,
    But we get joy from dancing in a loop,
Omega-shaped, then stretched out toward the future,
    Then with feet hunched again, forward we swoop.

Happy, we thrive, yet as we thrive we change!
    Alas, we'll soon turn into moths who fly
Uncalculated distances aloft,
    Infinite inches, up into the sky.

On that bright day, O God, may we remember
    Each journey always with one small step starts,
And trust that, though you once gave us but inches,
    You've dreams for us far greater than our hearts.

A Junebug's Jubilation

Shout hooray, all Junebug folk!
Have you heard (it's not a joke):
   We're the symbol of the Resurrection?
In an ancient pyramid
Where some royal mummies hid
   Were images of us in carved perfection!

Why? It was the simple fact
We play dead when we're attacked,
   Then we "rise again" when danger's passed!
"Scarab" is our family name,
Thus the charm is called the same,
   Bringing luck and safety unsurpassed!

But, alas, our mummies lay
Dead as doornails in decay!
   They'd no Easter Morn to cheer the grievers.
Still, to rapture we are drawn!
We give hope when hope is gone!
   Buoying up the hearts of brave believers!

The Rendezvous of a Kangaroo

When I consider how I'm odd
In how I look and move, dear God,
An awkward hopping kangaroo
Without a prayer to offer You,
    I raise my forepaws, bent and frail,
    To show I'm thankful for my days,
    Then leaning on my stubby tail
    I kick both feet in solemn praise.

I think you smile to see my fears:
My pointed snout, my upright ears,
My furry form some six feet tall
(With cousins but six inches small.)
    Do you delight in me today,
    Hip-hopping till my feet are sore?
    Grant at my death, at last I may
    Hop in your pouch forevermore.

The Ladybug's Lament

Forgive me, God, for crying out,
    you're not the one to blame,
You know the curse that saddens me:
    the burden of my name.
Yes I was born a "Ladybug"
    but of the male persuasion,
My world is all female defined
    no matter the occasion!

They own the church, they run the world,
    they credit or condemn,
They make a mess, then ask us males
    to clean it up for them.
They think of You as female too!
    Believe me, that's the worst.
A female God makes males a joke,
    invisible and cursed.

Dear God, give them new eyes to see
  how you gave double powers
To solve the puzzles of the world
  and make creation ours.
The sexes are not opposite,
  just different, not the same,
Males bring new genius, and new strength,
  and not just a new name.

Sexism is a brutal sin
  and leaves us males accurs'd,
How would the ladies like it
  if our roles were reversed?
They'd curse like fiends and then explode
  like nitroglycerin,
So let them sweat it not if we
  get strident now and then.

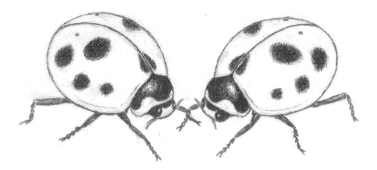

The Lyric
of a Meadowlark

I sing above the anger of the wind,
    I shout above the anguish of the sea,
Such are my prayers—for I belong to you,
    Earthmother Home, and you belong to me.

I am a part of all the wind's just wrath,
    I am a part of all the ocean's pain,
Their mighty voices rise like a common cry:
    Where is compassion? Where does justice reign?

Turning I see the sun caress a hillside
    Wild with a thousand flowers and children's play,
So I sing joy, and thankfulness, and wonder,
    As all creation teaches me to pray.

Like Shakespeare's lark "at break of day arising
    From sullen earth to sing at heaven's gate,"
First it is sorrow, then it's joy I'm singing,
    Just a small voice but part of something great.

The Headache of a Nuthatch

Please explain, dear God of Light,
Why it's so hard to know what's right,
  Why it's so tough for birds like me
  To crack the nuts of mystery.

Yes, I am famous from my youth
For heady searches for the truth,
  Chestnut or acorn, none's too tough,
  If I just smack it hard enough.

Using my bill for a hatchet blade,
Wham! and it's cracked, its wealth displayed,
  Yes, but meanwhile my head's in pain,
  Eyes that won't focus, neck with a sprain.

Why, when the thirst for wisdom wakes,
Knowledge such bloody entrance makes?
  Why hide the truth that life should teach
  Under a shell, so out of reach?

Nuthatchers ask—but Silence reigns,
All we can do is bruise our brains,
　　Bashing our beaks through hull and husk,
　　Hunting sweet wisdom, dawn to dusk.

Ode of an Octopus

Eight tentacles I'll raise
To our Creator's praise
  Who's made us Octopi so wondrous rare:
My three hearts throb and beat
With grateful love complete
  For Mother Ocean and her circling care.

Our suction cups hold tight
To prey or parasite
  While we, with pointed beaks, begin to pray
With thanks for clams and snails
Squid, shrimp, and lobster tails:
  A perfect seafood dinner every day.

At birth, we're quite petite,
At death, stretch thirty feet,
    And making love ranks high among our stunts,
We're fifty kinds, they say,
And sometimes we will lay
    One hundred eighty thousand eggs at once.

Some look at us and shriek
Because we're so unique,
    And call us Devilfish! But they don't think!
Could any but God's pet
Evade each mortal threat
    By disappearing into clouds of ink?

Attackers we confuse,
Then suddenly change hues!
    Blue, brown, pink, purple, red or white or gray!
Amazing! Thus we be
Evangelists for Thee:
    The very thought of us makes people pray!

Our great bright eyes explore
The deepest ocean floor
    Where your Dark Mystery glimmers unsurpassed,
We trust you'll not forsake us
Till age and death shall take us
    Into your cosmic hugging arms at last.

A Penitent Parrot's Apology

I hide my head beneath my wings,
    I'm guilty as can be,
I've sinned against the human race—
    By vice and gluttony.

I've blurted out into the air
    Words said in privacy!
And all for a cracker, nut, or crumb
    Which I swallow shamelessly.

My thick, hooked bill would make you think
    I'd keep my voice down low,
But no! When listeners come my way
    I crow out all I know.

The worst words that my masters speak
    Come tripping off my chin,
Dark curses said in secrecy
    Become a public sin.

See my face! It's red with shame,
  My feathers, a rainbow gown!
To indicate my penitence,
  I'm dressed up like a clown.

I'm so ashamed! Forgive me, God,
  More gossip I won't spread!
I'll keep all secrets from now on!
  (Hey, did you hear what the pope just said?)

A Querulous Quail's Request

Hear my voice in the meadow, Mother Nature,
　　My "bobwhite" is the prayer I sing on high,
I call out optimistically at dawning
　　To rally all the quail who are nearby.

How we love to feast together in the sunshine,
　　Finding blessings under every rock and shed,
Till the hunters hear us pray a bit too loudly
　　And disturb our peace with bullets,
　　shot, and lead!

Forgive if we're querulous or fretful,
　　Ill-tempered, cranky, snappish, or high-strung,
We regret to seem irascible and grouchy,
　　We just hate to lose our life when we are young.

Still the wise accept mortality as given,
　　And the Bible says your life lasts but a day,
So we ask the grace to have more faith and wisdom,
　　And try not to quail
　　when hunters come our way.

The Whisper of a Raccoon

Are you wondering who this is, My God?
    Shh! I'll speak quietly. Keep your voice low.
I am the Masked Raccoon, thief of the garden,
    Living in the woods incognito.

My father was an outlaw thief before me,
    My mother made her living on the sly,
All our family wear these masks across our faces
    So we're tough to capture or identify.

Yet you're clever, Great Detective Spirit,
    You're masked like me and hard to apprehend
As you sneak about earth working your wonders,
    All but invisible to foe or friend.

One secret: See this tail that hangs behind me,
    Almost a foot of rings and bushy hair?
If I get lost, just use my tail to find me,
    You'll know the rest of me's not far from there.

Although I live to snitch ripe corn and apples,
    And pilfer juicy loot from field and farm,
I'm grateful, God, your kindness gave me cunning
    To wear a mask that keeps me safe from harm.

Snoozetime for a Snail

Sleepy I am. I start to close my eyes,
Then climb inside my shell with soft goodbyes
    To all my deep-sea kin; and now to You,
    O God Most Wet, I'll say—a toodle-loo.

It's been a hectic day, a hectic week!
Racing to get somewhere, still up a creek
    Without a paddle, fingers, fins, or jet!
    I ask you, God, how hopeless can one get?

What have I done today? Well, nothing much,
Just family visits, daily prayers, and such,
    With long sea miles to go before I sleep.
    (I hope my relatives won't call me a creep!)

I've eighty thousand kinds of snails to greet,
Some up to 2 feet long, with giant feet
    Walking on mucus which we first exude,
    Then slide our feet along: It's rather crude.

Now I'll slow down. Ah, time at last to rest
Unwind, be calm and placid, still—and blest,
    Tucking myself in bed within the shell
    I've backpacked for myself. All shall be well.

The Turkey's Distress

Look down, Holy Mystery, Creator,
  I hope you have love in your eye:
It's Turkey, the jerk of the barnyard,
  Ashamed I'm so slow-brained and shy.

Though I am no beauty to look at,
    I've even more shameful insides,
Afraid to be known for a turkey,
    A creature that gobbles and hides.

Fenced in with superior creatures,
    I suffer stage fright to a fault,
Forgetting the few things I've mastered,
    My aching brain grinds to a halt.

As each year's Thanksgiving approaches,
    I pray: Let me die and be meat!
And manage at last to give pleasure,
    At least I was useful to eat!

Look down, Holy Mystery, Creator:
    I'm a clown feeling awkward and shy,
Why create such ridiculous creatures?
    Don't answer! I'll trust you know why.

The Un-Prayer
of a Unicorn

Since I'm just an imaginary animal,
    I'll offer this imaginary prayer:
O Imaginary Lord, with your non-existent sword,
    Do away with Evil Beings everywhere!

Crush the proud who imagine they're immortal!
    Save the humble who imagine they are lost!
Come, Imaginary Sire, bless the nations you inspire
    With imaginary fire on Pentecost.

This poor unicorn is helpless here before you,
    Just the mere imagination of a horse
With a single horn of magic and a story that is tragic
    But without a true reality, of course.

But, real God! Unimaginary Spirit!
   Womb of Being, Thou to whom real creatures pray,
Could you give me one tiny spark of being?
   Work your magic! Don't you do it every day?

The Vow of the Benevolent Vulture

While I am justly proud
I'm not one of the crowd
   Who scoffs at every creature who excels,
I disavow one role:
The vulture in my soul
   With expertise on everything that smells.

It may be in my glands
To take contemptuous stands
    At lesser birds I easily surpass,
But I am sick to death
Of that disdainful breath
    That scoffs at those perceived as second class.

Instead I'd soar above,
An expert on "wide love,"
    A vulture with compassion! There's a twist!
I'll vow to lose the skill
Of how to maim and kill:
    Become instead a pure philanthropist.

Good God of Earth and stars,
Have pity on my scars
    That make me scornful, harsh, and insecure,
May prayers of this poor vulture
Produce a kinder culture
    With a preferential option for the poor!

The Worried Worm's Conversion

Behold me, God of Endless Peace and Calm,
 I fret, catastrophize, worry, and fear,
Expect disaster, wince at threatening clouds,
 Squirm this way, that way, feeling doom is near.

The earth feels cold, my churning stomach aches:
 I'll never do the charities I should!
It's late and I've got almost nothing done!
 Dear God, you'd think by now I'd understood.

What? Well, that we are worthless, useless worms
 Until we till this earth from shore to shore,
That's what an earthworm's job it is to do,
 What else on earth did you create us for?

To laugh? You're kidding, God? You speak in jest!
 To love? Enjoy? Thrive? You are making fun!
We live to labor, don't we, Holy One?
 No? Then I'm just a hopeless simpleton!

I'll start from scratch: I'll turn and love myself
　　Before I crawl or wiggle or turn earth,
Perhaps a worm is miracle enough,
　　Without the need to prove a sacred worth.

How great! The world's weight is off my back!
　　I'll learn to love, my native grace affirm,
Become more catholic in my taste for life,
　　And laugh at silly worries of a worm.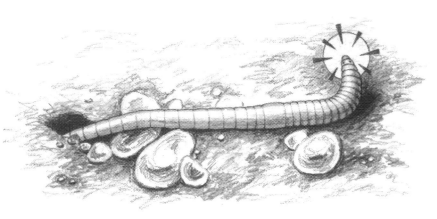

The Xema's Dream

In case you don't know,
We're a gull white as snow
    Except for our hood and our pack,
We're a bit like a skunk
Or a old-fashioned monk
    In a robe that's half white and half black.

You, God of the cold,
Gave us hearts that are bold
    So we fly to the Arctic to breed,
And although love is slow
When it's 90 below
    We have managed somehow to succeed.

We adore the outdoors
When the arctic wind roars
    And declares it is time to find mates,
So we fly toward the cold
For we've always been told
    That's where joyous communion awaits.

Tell us, God of the Chosen,
Is heaven all frozen
    With ice that's as hard as cement?
Just as long as there's love
In that Arctic Above,
    We will live there forever content.

The Anguish of an Angelic Yak

I'm the trucker of the mountains,
I'm a fountain of fresh milk,
   I'm the heater of the huts Tibetans make,
When I get too old to travel
Or to carry wine and silk
   I'll become their boots and sweaters,
       and their steak.

Yaks are happy to be useful,
Yaks are tickled to be loved,
    Yaks are quite content to end up in a pot,
But, dear God of crowded alleys
Where we're rudely pushed and shoved,
    What our masters call us daily, we are not!

Blockheads, dummies, nerds, they name us,
Numskulls, dimwits, stupid jerks!
    Move your lazy bones, they shout at kindly yaks!
Devil! Monster! Clod! they call us,
Nincompoop! dope! dunce! the works!
    Every awful name is laid upon our backs!

We're refined! Urbane! Artistic!
We're creative with high claims!
    We're a blessing from on high—but no one cares!
So, dear Manager of Heaven,
Teach all people who call "names"—
    They may be cursing angels unawares.

A Compliant
Zebra's Complaint

Please excuse me, God, I'm angry and indignant,
    Here I stand looking silly as can be,
We were told to get ready for a party!
    And to dress up for a jungle jamboree!

So black zebras got white stripes to wrap around 'em
    And the whites wore stripes of black to make
        'em weird,
So by dressing for a party—accidentally
    All our zebra disagreements disappeared!

Where's the party? Where's the costumes
        for the others?
    Where's the lions wearing snowshoes
            and tall hats?
Where's the vultures and turtles
        in their technicolor girdles?
    Where's the wedding gowns for porcupines
            and bats?

Yes, some snakes and birds are dressed
  for celebration,
  For the rest, I think, new costumes are a must,
And the great effect we're after
  is a lot more friendly laughter
  That will give the jungle far more peace and trust.

So, dear God, we beg, please populate the jungle
  With comic clowns and droll comediennes,
When we fill our mouths with chuckles
  and with snickers,
  We're less prone to make a meal
  out of our friends.

Author's Notes

Animals can be healing—at least that's my experience. This book's Introduction explains what I mean. Each animal is a "word" of God: peculiar, mysterious, purposeful, awe-inspiring. In the foregoing psalms the bugs and beasts turn to God in prayer, and can guide us in our prayers as well. The following notes draw out the implications of their psalms for our own health and healing.

Armadillo: In time of pain and disappointment, I find it soothing to think about God's caring love and presence. So does the armadillo. The most fundamental fact in life is that we live within the love of the Divine Wisdom that created and holds in being all that is. The world may seem dangerous—but at the most basic level all is well. We are cared for.

Butterfly: Death may be easier to think about if we consider it a part of life, a part of nature. The short-lived butterfly can be a healing symbol of courage in the face of death. To live as the butterfly does—in harmony with nature—is a healthy ideal. In the light of faith, perhaps we can see our death as part of our life, not its end.

Chicken: The prayer of the chicken soothes my spirit when I feel like a "chicken." It helps me realize that God is not far away, or unsympathetic to my worries. In fact, the Divine Mystery is surely very close, and knows and cares about me in every detail of my scary life. That medicinal thought gives me at least a little courage.

Dragonfly: Here's a wonderful thought: to think of oneself as "Wisdom's Child." And that is what we are. God may be called "Wisdom" because in creation we constantly find—right in the middle of mystery—evidence of intelligence, wise design, harmony, patterned growth, and purposefulness. When depression attacks, I find that healthy thoughts—like thinking of oneself as Wisdom's Child—can be good medicine.

Elephant: How do people put up with the heavy burdens of illness, physical challenges, or debilitating accidents? In thousands of ways. This elephant just says "Amen." So be it. Let it be. Thy will be done. Within limits, this is a healthy approach. It avoids despair, or blaming God, or a destructive anger. Accepting God's Way is also a hope for better things in the future. In God's good time.

Firefly: Perspective is crucial. Most of us humans are at least a little afraid of the dark. How strange and foolish that seems to a firefly! How many of our other fears are foolish? Some must be. Perhaps there are whole classes or nations of people we fear. How bizarre an illusion! The firefly opens us to the unexpected!

Goat: There is healing in the humble goat who buckles down to the work before him while keeping all his dreams alive. We are never soul-healthy if a few dreams—even impossible dreams—are not alive in our hearts. We are made for greatness. The task is to become who we are meant to be—in God's dreams.

Hummingbird: Thoughts of the hummingbird heal our hearts when we see what joy and glory can enrich the lives of those considered small and powerless. Creation has a place and a role for each creature, even ourselves. I don't have wings to flap at 70 times a second, but with help from other humans, I can fly, I can build skyscrapers, I can create a communications highway, I can design melodies that heal and medicines that give life. I can build a love that's eternal. (That's something to hum about.)

Inchworm: There is healing peace of soul in thinking "the last shall be first, and the first last." Most of us feel (don't we?) that we will personally make out well by that prediction: We feel among "the last." I'm God's inchworm, we can say. Today I go inch by inch, but big things lie ahead! God has no small dreams.

Junebug: I love the scarab image because it stands for a belief shared by all the religions of the earth: life after death. For me, everything points toward some kind of permanent existence. It gives meaning to so much that otherwise appears to be meaningless and absurd. It enables us to carry on when other hopes and dreams don't come true. It's essential medicine—as long as it doesn't shut down our efforts to achieve a just society in this world.

Kangaroo: It is always healthy for me to try to see myself through the eyes of God. Somehow that caring gaze smoothes down my jangled nerves, reduces my worry level, draws me together. Before the eyes of God I need not keep up my pretenses. There I am utterly known, and loved, as I am. I may be as mistaken in my notion of God as is the kangaroo who longs to jump back into

God-Mother's pouch. Still something about that desire is profoundly right.

Ladybug: There is an anguish abroad among all oppressed groups, especially women. Systemic sexism wherever it is found—in law, in language, in prejudice, in church life—causes profound distress and cripples our society. Imaginatively reversing sex roles can be enlightening. And with a little twist of humor, healing.

Meadowlark: I find the wonderful little up-down song of the meadowlark healing music therapy. "I've both grief and joy to sing," it seems to say. That song convinces me that the world is largely benevolent—as does the welcoming blueness of the sky, and encouraging green of earth. Add to this a lark's song. A superb setting for human life!

Nuthatch: Life is difficult, but every nuthatch lives the lesson that persistence wins out. We know in ourselves—and in evolution—an all-embracing drive toward life, growth, fertility, and improvement. From another perspective that force is just our unseen Magnetic Divinity, drawing all things inexorably toward itself. Perhaps in our lives we need less stress management and just more struggle motivation.

Octopus: We are all more or less blinded by illusions of different kinds. Certainly I am. The God of this octopus heals one illusion: that God is "tame." The Divine Being is wilder, spookier, and more impossibly mysterious than we can even imagine. One long look deep into the ocean is proof of that. Go there for octopus medicine if you feel out of touch with the depths of the Holy Mystery around us.

Parrot: "To err is human, to forgive, divine": I was never really taught this profound bit of wisdom. My heroes were all superhuman, my monarch God ultimately unforgiving. So the Penitent Parrot helps me laugh at my delusion that I can or should be perfect, or have the ability to judge others or even myself. God loves basket-cases too!

Quail: I know that many of my fears are unfounded and exaggerated. What to do? Consider this quail. Yes, fear of death is our primary, fundamental fear—but just as enlightened religion can deal healingly with death, often it can deal healingly with fear. There are worse things than death. If quail can stop quivering about it, so can I.

Raccoon: Raccoon medicine makes me laugh at my own silly masks—which so often accomplish nothing, only make me look peculiar. Do you find yourself wearing masks occasionally—of the faultless saint (when we rush to judge human failure), of the problem-free genius (when we're eager to impress)? The strange thing is that almost everyone can see right through our masks, even children. And God.

Snail: Apparently even snails find some times in their life quite hectic. Dairy cows—reputedly "contented"—are in fact prone to stress (which cuts down their milk production). From all of which we can take a therapeutic lesson. Unremitting "striving" is not a human ideal. Lightheartedness is. Snail medicine consists of half whimsy and half self-respect. Slow down. Unwind. Relax. Smile. Lose a race or two, and unburden your heart of every need to be first.

Turkey: This turkey was and is a strongly healing image for me—as I explained in the Introduction. Once I was aware of how turkey-like I was feeling, it made me laugh. The sweet balm of laughter can often soothe one's irritated self-image. Why we take ourselves so seriously is a mystery. It invariably leads to sadness. And catching oneself at it can lead to laughter.

Unicorn: When we feel low (unloved, unsuccessful, or confused), we can at least rejoice that we exist. We're each a miracle: a living, breathing miracle. Why miraculous? Because we have being—and that means God is caringly pouring existence into us at every moment, giving us the magic of existence and vitality. From the perspective of a merely imaginary animal like the unicorn, that is something amazingly wonderful.

Vulture: I find it healing to name and acknowledge a shadow side of my self whenever I discover it. One of my shadowy selves is a snob: "one who is convinced of and flaunts his supposed superiority." The snob is a great critic of everything in sight, like a vulture with expertise on everything that smells. Vulture medicine builds up compassion; cures snobbishness.

Worm: Who lays those illusory "ideals" on us? And who convinces us of our ultra-unworthy performance? A twisted, inhuman spirituality can do it. It can keep pulling the ideals ever higher, and our self-esteem ever lower, until we tighten up and squirm like a worried worm. Humanize your goals. Appreciate yourself.

Xema: There is no making rules for love. When one is gripped by love, reasoning and logic seem irrelevant. What is more, a parent's love for a child or a lover's fascination with a beloved is probably life's most powerful epiphany of the presence of the Divine. "God is love." It's altogether awesome.

Yak: Why are names so important? Because they often carry along a world of suggestion. Many a child has come home devastated because of being "called a name." Having unfair, cruel names for whole groups of innocent people is like a cancer on our culture. Remember the yak when anyone puts you down. Yak medicine moderates cruel judgments, and assuages a sharp tongue.

Zebra: When I take a good look at a zebra, I am inclined to say to God: "Come on, you can't be serious!" And that's just it: Obviously there are times when even God can't be serious. Only a costume designer with a limitless imagination could put together a zebra suit. That's one healing thought. Another is the question of whether zebras have black stripes or white stripes. Perspective makes the deciding difference. Just so, every human face is colored.

Afterword by Noah

Dear Reader: As you might imagine, I am very pleased with these prayers. How far my animal friends have come since they paraded off my ark into the soggy and devastated world!

And I am very honored to be writing this Afterword. I felt sure Noah was a forgotten name, and my good old Ark a lost story. But, thanks to Elephant, I'm not forgotten. And thanks to Mrs. Meadowlark and the search committee, I was found. (Gone fishing, of course.)

What a zoo that ark was!

The Lord God had commanded me to build accommodations for seven pairs of clean animals and seven unclean, plus pairs of seven kinds of birds. Which I did. Ha! Wonderful plans! When the weather turned bad, and the Deluge was clearly on its way, I called aboard my sons and their wives.

Then I called in all my closest animal friends, just 21 couples, as God had said—but they brought their relatives! That part never got into the text of Genesis. I couldn't refuse them. And we ran out of everything—while it rained dogs and cats for 40 days and 40 nights! Then it took another 150 days until the waters fell!

Meanwhile everybody got bored and wanted to begin propagating. I said: Wait! Not yet! Every animal pair waited —except the fleas: and then we had a circus, you can imagine.

What a grand delight was debarkation, a day to remember. Since then, wonderful new animals have evolved. I am so proud of them.

In my opinion this compendium of prayers from animals creates a new high-water mark in Critter Spirituality. Special thanks to the one who recorded and collected them. He and his prayers inspire us all.

Other books by Bill Cleary...

In God's Presence
Centering Experiences for Circles and Solitudes

For each prayer experience Cleary uses a centering technique to help readers move into a meditative attitude. Then he offers a reflection and a Scripture citation, a prayer from a world religion and, finally, a psalm.

ISBN: 0-89622-608-5, 144 pp, $9.95

Psalm Services for Group Prayer

Each of the 36 services includes an opening prayer and psalm, as well as a Gospel reading. There is also time for prayer, when members of the group are invited to voice their joys and concerns.

ISBN: 0-89622-526-7, 96 pp, $9.95

Psalm Services for Parish Meetings

The ancient psalms of David form the basis for half the prayers in this book, with the other half featuring original psalms written by the author.

ISBN: 0-89622-510-0, 96 pp, $9.95

Available at religious bookstores or from

TWENTY-THIRD PUBLICATIONS

P.O. Box 180 • Mystic, CT 06355
1-800-321-0411